# Space Hunt

James Noble • Jonatronix

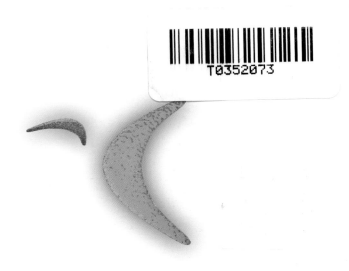

T0352073

OXFORD

UNIVERSITY PRESS

# Max's mission log

We are travelling through space on board the micro-ship Excelsa with our new friends, Nok and Seven.

We're on a mission to save Planet Exis (Nok's home planet), which is running out of power. We need to collect four fragments that have been hidden throughout the Beta-Prime Galaxy. Together the fragments form the Core of Exis. Only the Core will restore power to the planet.

It's not easy. A space villain called Badlaw wants the power of the Core for himself. His army of robotic Krools is never far behind us!

**Fragments collected so far: 3**

# The Beta-Prime Galaxy
## Destination: Planet Moxor

### Planet Moxor

### Planet fragment

**Planet landscape**

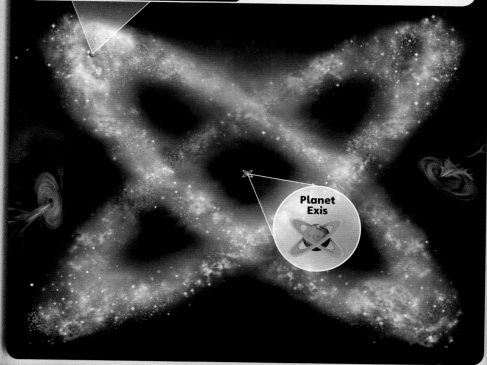

Planet Exis

# Chapter 1 – Mission Moxor

"We should arrive at Planet Moxor in twenty minutes," said Cat, turning round to face Max.

Max drummed his fingers on his desk. He couldn't wait to get to Moxor, find the final fragment and complete their mission.

"Our data shows that Moxor is a hostile planet," said Seven.

"Searching for the fragment could be tough then," added Ant.

Nok looked round at his friends. "We can't give up now," he said. "We need all four fragments to save Planet Exis."

"Don't worry," Max promised. "We're not turning back now we've come this far."

# Planet Moxor

Planet Moxor is a desert planet. It is home to some of the deadliest plants in the galaxy. It has one stretch of water, the Sea Stripe, that runs right round its centre. It has three suns!

## Known life forms

▶ Moxorians

▶ Grumptus plants

## Surface conditions

▶ Very hot and dry

▶ Rocky desert

▶ Cliffs

**dry, rocky desert** ●●○○○○○○○○○○○○○○○○○

**Sea Stripe** ●●○○○○○○○○○○

**cliffs** ●●○○○○○

Just then, a warning alarm filled the bridge.
It sounded like the loudest siren in
the universe.

"**DANGER ... DANGER ...**" said the ship.

Tiger looked at the front viewscreen. "I
can't see anything."

Cat studied her scanners. "Me neither."

"Wait," she said, with a gasp. A large shape began to pulse on the screen. "Krool ship coming in fast!" she cried.

Badlaw's metallic army had been hunting the friends relentlessly. Badlaw wanted the fragments, too. If he got his claws on them, he would be able to control the whole galaxy.

# Chapter 2 – Spotted!

Seven tapped at a control panel to override the alarm. It finally went quiet.

"I'm getting a message coming in," said Ant.
He pressed a button on his desk and an image appeared on the viewscreen. It was Krool 1, commander of the Krools. "Crew of the Excelsa," he said, "surrender or be destroyed!"

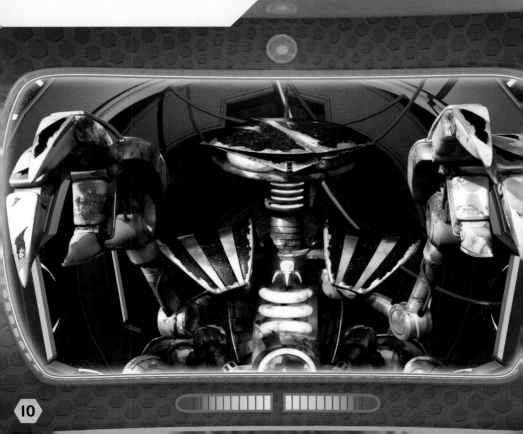

Krool 1 vanished from the screen.

"What options do we have?" asked Max.

"We could try to outrun them," suggested Tiger.

"Ship, what are our chances?" Max asked.

"***Outcome uncertain***," replied the ship.

"We have to try!" said Nok.

Max thought for a moment. "Tiger's right. Our best chance is to try to get to Moxor before the Krools. We might be able to lose them on the planet."

"How can we outrun them? They're bigger than us," Cat said worriedly.

"I have an idea," Tiger said, "but it's risky." They turned to face him.

"We can divert more power to the engines," said Tiger. "That will give us enough power to accelerate beyond level 5 and outrun the Krools."

Ant gasped. "But that means turning off the ship's shields!"

"We'll be sitting space-ducks if the Krools attack," Cat said.

"It's the only chance we have," said Max. "Tiger, get down to the engine room and get to work."

"I'll need some help," Tiger replied.

"I'll go," said Ant, quickly.

Ant and Tiger ran to the transit-tube.

Seven rushed after them. "Wait for me! I'd better come, too."

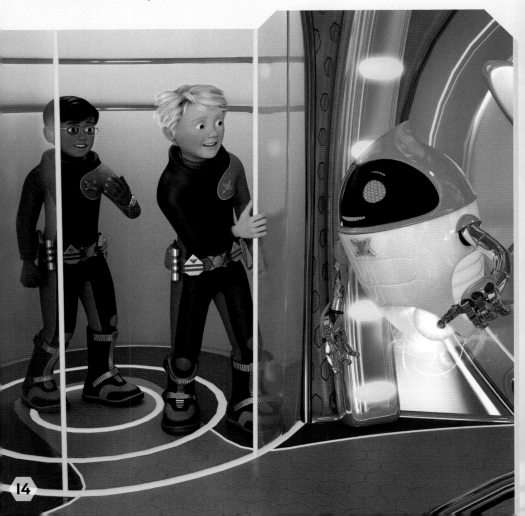

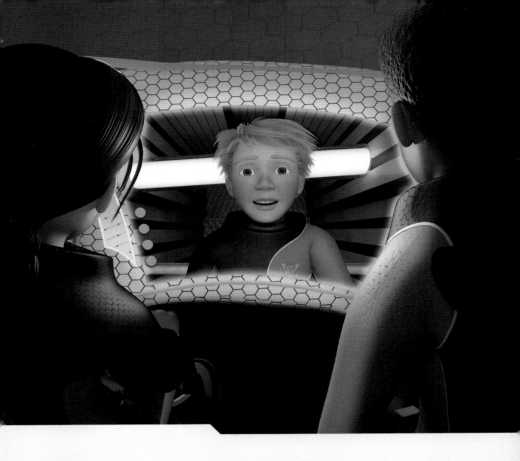

Minutes ticked by. Max and Cat stayed glued
to the scanners. It seemed to be taking Ant,
Tiger and Seven a long time to divert the
power, and the Krools' ship was getting
ever closer.

Finally, the lights on the bridge flashed
and then dimmed to a red glow. Tiger's face
appeared on the communi-screen. "Power
diverted," he grinned.

"Here goes," said Max, slipping into Ant's seat. He accelerated past level 5.

"I really hope this works," Nok said, as he heard the ship's engines rumble and whir.

Cat saw the stars outside become thick, white streaks. "Wow!" she gasped.

"*WARNING!*" said the ship. "*Continuing at this speed will result in complete engine failure. One minute until engine failure.*"

"How far are we from Moxor?" asked Max.

Cat ran back to her chair. "Four minutes," she said.

Max looked at her nervously. They were not going to make it.

*"**Thirty seconds until engine failure**."*

"We've got to slow down!" Nok yelled.

Tiger appeared on the communi-screen. He was surrounded by steam. "The engines are overheating!" he shouted.

*"**Fifteen seconds until engine failure**."*

"Max? What shall we do?" cried Cat.

Max pulled the lever on the control panel. The ship began to slow.

# Chapter 3 – Space junk

The noise of the engines faded to a low rumble.

Ahead, Max noticed a stream of space junk. "The ship should be small enough to hide in there," he said. "Take us in, Nok."

Nok guided the ship into the space junk. He weaved his way through the floating debris until the ship was deep inside the river of rubbish.

Max spoke into the communi-screen. "Tiger, cut all the power to the engines."

"WHAT?" Tiger cried.

"The Krools can't fly their massive ship through all this rubbish," Max explained. "There's no way they'll find us."

Cat hoped he was right.

The ship became completely silent.

Cat checked the scanners. "The Krools are close," she said.

"Don't worry. We're safe here," Max reassured her.

"We can't stay here forever," said Cat.

"We only need to stay long enough for the Krools to think we've got away," he replied.

They waited for what seemed like an eternity.
Then, suddenly, they saw some lime-green
shapes whizz past the viewscreen.

"What are they?" asked Cat.

The shapes zoomed back past.

Max frowned. "Are those ... *boomerangs*?"

"They're heat-seeking gel boomerangs,"
cried Nok.

"Tiger, Ant!" Max cried. "Turn the engines back on! We have to get out of here NOW!"

With a giant whir, the micro-ship came back to life.

"Let's go!" yelled Nok, as he zoomed the ship away from the boomerangs.

# Chapter 4 – Dodging the boomerangs

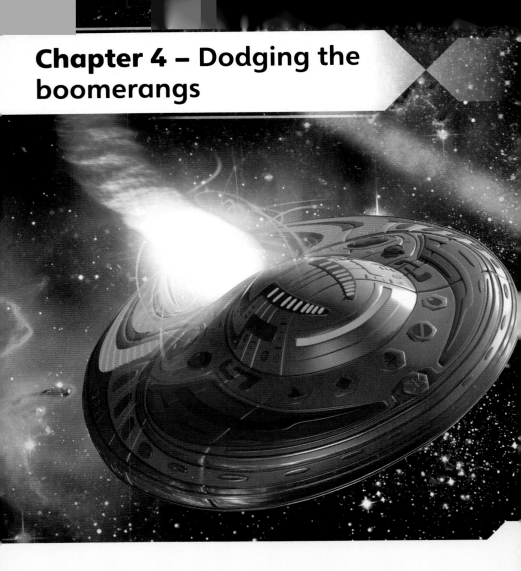

Two boomerangs were spinning their way through the space junk after them.

Nok moved the ship hard to the left …

… then sharply to the right …

… but the boomerangs just got closer.

"Hold on," yelled Nok, pulling back on the steering orbs.

The ship shot up, then backwards into a loop the loop. As the ship swept out of the way, the boomerangs slammed into each other, creating a storm of sticky green bubbles.

Nok punched the air. "We're safe!"

Tiger appeared on the screen. "Did we get away?"

Cat looked again at the scanner. "No," she yelled. "Another boomerang is on its way."

Nok's face fell.

"How far to Moxor?" asked Max.

"We'll be there in one minute," replied Cat.

The boomerang caught them up in no time. Nok pulled desperately at the steering orbs, making the ship spin sideways, over and over.

Suddenly ... *THWAP*! The boomerang slammed right into them. The ship was trapped in the sticky gel.

Max thought quickly. "Maybe we can melt our way out of this!" he said. He gripped the lever and pushed the ship back past level 5.

Nok pulled at the steering orbs with all his strength. His arms strained and beads of sweat ran down his face. "It's no good!" he cried.

"*Ten seconds until engine failure*," said the ship.

Just then, the gel started to melt. The micro-ship blasted free.

"*Entering Moxor's atmosphere now*," the ship announced.

"Tiger, Ant, Seven," said Max. "You'd better get back up to the bridge. We'll be landing soon."

There was no response.

"Guys?" said Cat, peering at the communi-screen.

The engine room was empty. Their friends were gone.

Find out what happens next in
*The Deadly Cave.*